Contents

Interstitial Cystitis

What is interstitial cystitis?

Interstitial cystitis (IC) is a complex condition that is identified by chronic inflammation of the bladder muscle layers, which produces the following symptoms:

• pelvic and abdominal pain and pressure

• frequent urination

• urgency (feeling like you need to urinate, even right after urinating)

• incontinence (accidental leakage of urine)

Discomfort can range from a mild burning sensation to severe pain. The degree of discomfort can be persistent or infrequent. Some people have periods of remission.

According to the Interstitial Cystitis Association, IC affects more than 12 million people in the United States. Women are most likely to develop IC, but children and adult men can get it as well.

IC is also known as painful bladder syndrome (PBS), bladder pain syndrome (BPS), and chronic pelvic pain (CPP).

What are the symptoms of IC?

You may experience one or more of the following symptoms:

• chronic or intermittent pain in the pelvis

• pelvic pressure or discomfort

• urinary urgency (feeling that you need to urinate)

• frequent urination day and night

• pain during sexual intercourse

Your symptoms may vary from day to day, and you may experience periods when you are symptom-free. Symptoms may worsen if you develop a urinary tract infection.

What causes IC?

The exact cause of IC isn't known, but researchers postulate that several factors may damage the lining of the bladder and therefore trigger the disorder. These include:

• trauma to the bladder lining (for example, from surgical procedures)

• excessive stretching of the bladder, usually due to long periods without a bathroom break

• weakened or dysfunctional pelvic floor muscles

12

- autoimmune disorders

- repeated bacterial infections

- hypersensitivity or inflammation of pelvic nerves

- spinal cord trauma

Many people with IC also have irritable bowel syndrome (IBS) or fibromyalgia. Some researchers believe that IC may be part of a generalized inflammatory disorder that affects multiple organ systems.

Researchers are also investigating the possibility that people may inherit a genetic predisposition to IC. Although it's not common, IC has been reported in blood relatives. Cases have been seen in mother and daughter as well as in two or more sisters.

Research is ongoing to determine the cause of IC and to develop more effective treatments.

How is IC diagnosed?

There are no tests that make a definitive diagnosis of IC, so many cases of IC go undiagnosed. Because IC shares many of the same symptoms of other bladder disorders, your doctor needs to rule these out first. These other disorders include:

• urinary tract infections

• bladder cancer

• chronic prostatitis (in men)

• chronic pelvic pain syndrome (in men)

• endometriosis (in women)

You'll be diagnosed with IC once your doctor determines that your symptoms aren't due to one of these disorders.

powered by Rubicon Project

Potential complications of IC

IC can cause several complications, including:

• reduced bladder capacity due to stiffening of the bladder wall

• lower quality of life as a result of frequent urination and pain

• barriers to relationships and sexual intimacy

• issues with self-esteem and social embarrassment

• sleep disturbances

• anxiety and depression

How is IC treated?

There is no cure or definitive treatment for IC. Most people use a combination of treatments, and you may have to try several approaches before you settle on the therapy that provides the most relief. Following are some IC treatments.

Medication

Your doctor may prescribe one or more of the following drugs to help improve your symptoms:

• Pentosan polysulfate sodium (Elmiron) has been approved by the Food and Drug Administration to treat IC. Doctors don't know exactly how pentosan works, but it may help repair tears or defects in the bladder wall.

WARNING

• You should not take pentosan if you are pregnant or are planning to become pregnant.

• Nonsteroidal anti-inflammatories, including ibuprofen, naproxen, aspirin, and others, are taken for pain and inflammation.

16

- Tricyclic antidepressants (such as amitriptyline) help relax your bladder and also block pain.

- Antihistamines (such as Claritin) decrease urinary urgency and frequency.

Bladder distention

Bladder distention is a procedure that stretches the bladder using water or gas. It can help relieve symptoms in some people, possibly by increasing the capacity of the bladder and by interrupting pain signals transmitted by nerves in the bladder. It can take two to four weeks to notice improvement in your symptoms.

Bladder instillation

Bladder instillation involves filling the bladder with a solution containing dimethyl sulfoxide (Rimso-50), also called DMSO. The DMSO solution is held in the bladder for 10 to 15 minutes before it's emptied. One treatment cycle typically includes up to two treatments per week for six to eight weeks, and the cycle can be repeated as needed.

It's thought that the DMSO solution may reduce inflammation of the bladder wall. It may also prevent muscle spasms that cause pain, frequency, and urgency.

Electrical nerve stimulation

Transcutaneous electrical nerve stimulation (TENS) delivers mild electrical pulses through the skin to stimulate the nerves to the bladder. TENS may help relieve symptoms by increasing blood flow to the bladder, strengthening pelvic muscles that help control the bladder, or triggering the release of substances that block pain.

Diet

Many people with IC discover that specific foods and beverages make their symptoms worse. Common foods that may worsen IC include:

• alcohol

• tomatoes

• spices

• chocolate

• anything with caffeine

• acidic foods like citrus fruits and juices

Your doctor will help you to determine if you are sensitive to any foods or beverages.

Quitting smoking

Although there is no proven correlation between smoking and IC, smoking is definitely linked to bladder cancer. It's possible that quitting smoking may help lessen or relieve your symptoms.

Exercise

Maintaining an exercise routine may help you manage your symptoms. You may have to modify your routine so that you avoid high-impact activity that causes flare-ups. Try some of these workouts:

• yoga

• walking

• tai chi

• low-impact aerobics or Pilates

A physical therapist can teach you exercises to strengthen your bladder and pelvic muscles. Talk to your doctor about meeting with a physical therapist.

Bladder training

Techniques designed to lengthen the time between urinating may help relieve symptoms. Your doctor can discuss these techniques with you.

Stress reduction

Learning to deal with life's stresses and the stress of having IC may provide symptom relief. Meditation and biofeedback may also help.

Surgery

There are several surgical options to increase the size of the bladder and remove or treat ulcers in the bladder. Surgery is rarely used and is considered only when symptoms are severe and other treatments have failed to provide relief. Your doctor will discuss these options with you if you are a candidate for surgery.

Long-term outlook

There is no cure for IC. It can last for years or even a lifetime. The main goal of treatment is to find the combination of therapies that best provides long-term symptom relief.

Appetizers, Side Dishes, Seasonings, and Spreads

Lemon Vegetable Rice

Per Serving: 304.9 Calories ~ 6.2 G Protein ~ 50.4 G Carbohydrate ~ 3.2 G Fiber ~ 9.7 G

Total Fat ~ 1.6 G Saturated Fat ~ 0.0 Mg Cholesterol ~ 397.2 Mg Sodium

For all those zucchinis we gardeners don't know what to do with in the fall, this is a terrific, light side dish that goes well with any dinner.

Ingredients

- Juice of 2 medium lemons
- 2 tablespoons maple syrup
- 2 cups of organic chicken broth
- 1 cups of short-grain brown rice
- 1/2 teaspoon sea salt
- 1 cinnamon stick

- 5 whole cloves

- 2 tablespoons olive oil

- 1 teaspoon cumin seeds

- 1 small onion, thinly sliced

- 2 small zucchinis, sliced

- 1/3 cup roasted cashews, whole

- 2 tablespoons fresh sweet basil, chopped

- Lemon wedges for garnish

Instructions

-Pour lemon juice, maple syrup, and chicken broth into a saucepan; add rice, sea salt, cinnamon stick, and cloves.

-Cover, bring to a boil, and boil for 2 minutes. Reduce heat and simmer for 25-30 minutes or until all liquid has been absorbed.

-In a large skillet, saute cumin seeds in olive oil until they begin to pop. Add onion and cook for another 5 minutes over medium heat.

-Add zucchini and cashews, and saute until zucchini is tender.

-Stir in the basil and the rice, heat for another minute or two, and serve garnished with lemon wedges.

Serves 6-8.

Substitutions

if you prefer a different type of nut, i would suggest pine nuts. if you don't have fresh basil, you can use any other fresh herb or leave that ingredient out.

Mango Salsa

Per Serving: 79.1 Calories ~ 0.9 G Protein ~ 20.5 G Carbohydrate ~ 2.3 G Fiber ~ 0.3 G

Total Fat ~ 0.1 G Saturated Fat ~ 0.0 Mg Cholesterol ~ 3.3 Mg Sodium

Of all the tomato dishes, salsa proved the hardest one for me to give up; therefore I had to come up with an alternative. You can use this version to replace salsa in any dish and to add a whole new dimension of flavor. It's perfect over a mildly seasoned white fish such as halibut. It also can complement guacamole or any Mexican dish.

Ingredients

- 3 ripe mangos, peeled and diced
- 1 red onion, minced
- 4 tablespoons finely chopped cilantro

- Juice of 1/2 lemon

- 2 medium-spice peppers, such an Anaheim peppers (depending on your tolerance for spice)

- Sea salt to taste

- 1 medium red bell pepper, minced (optional)

Instructions

-Combine all ingredients in a large bowl. Serve immediately with rice crackers, or store in the refrigerator. After it sits in the refrigerator for a little while, it tastes even better.

Serves 6-8.

Substitutions

You can experiment with adding anything you want, e.g., black beans, green bell peppers, avocado. You can even try adding other fruit such as kiwis or nectarines. If you cannot tolerate spice, leave out the hot peppers; it still tastes great.

Healthy Tidbit

Because mangos are cooling, they are great thirst quenchers. Mangos are high in vitamin-A precursors and vitamin C and are also a good source of potassium, which can aid in cardiovascular health. Mangos can be toning to all body types and constitutions.

Mashed "Potatoes" (Mashed Jerusalem Artichokes)

Per Serving: 80.4 Calories ~ 1.8 G Protein ~ 13.5 G Carbohydrate ~ 1.3 G Fiber ~ 2.4 G

Total Fat ~ 0.3 G Saturated Fat ~ 0.0 Mg Cholesterol ~ 5.3 Mg Sodium

If you desire mashed potatoes at your Thanksgiving dinner, this is a great alternative.

Ingredients

- 1 pound Jerusalem artichokes, scrubbed

- 1 tablespoon olive oil

- 1 tablespoon fresh tarragon, chopped

- 2 tablespoons soy milk

- Sea salt and pepper to taste

Instructions

-Preheat oven to 400° F.

-Cut artichokes into wedges, toss with olive oil, and place in a baking pan. Bake for 35-40 minutes or until tender.

-Remove from oven, mash well or pass through a food processor, and add remaining ingredients. Stir once more and serve warm.

Serves 6.

Substitutions

If you have a favorite mashed potato recipe, try it with Jerusalem artichokes. Just make sure to use a milk substitute, unless you can tolerate a little dairy. You can also steam cauliflower and use it in place of the Jerusalem artichokes. In place of tarragon, try oregano and/or thyme.

Healthy Tidbit

Jerusalem artichokes are a superior source of inulin, which is a compound beneficial for diabetics. They contain pro-vitamin A, B-complex vitamins, potassium, iron, calcium, and magnesium. They have been known to relieve asthmatic conditions, treat constipation, and nourish the lungs. It is best to purchase them during fall and winter, when their flavor peaks.

Milk Thistle Seasoning Salt

This blend is a tasty—and healthier—alternative to plain salt.

Ingredients

- 3 tablespoons milk thistle seeds (you can find these at a health-food store)
- 3 tablespoons sea salt

Instruction

-Grind the milk thistle seeds in a coffee grinder until you have a fine powder. Mix with sea salt. Use as a replacement for regular salt.

Substitutions

Adding dried seaweed will afford even more nutrients. Just grind the seaweed in the coffee grinder and add the powder to the above mixture.

Healthy Tidbit

Milk thistle is specific in treating the liver, spleen, and kidneys. It is a very powerful protectant of the liver and is indicated for weak veins, blood stasis, and liver diseases. The liver is an important organ of detoxification.

Olive Oil-Butter Spread

Per Serving: 107.7 Calories ~ 0.1 G Protein ~ 0.0 G Carbohydrate ~ 0.0 G Fiber ~ 12.2 G

Total Fat ~ 5.5 G Saturated Fat ~ 20.4 Mg Cholesterol ~ 54.6 Mg Sodium

I learned about this blend from my mentor, Dr. Dick Thom, who inspired this cookbook. Use it as a spread instead of plain organic butter or in cooking in place of plain organic olive oil.

Ingredients

- 1 pound organic butter, softened
- 1 cup extra-virgin olive oil

Instructions

-If necessary, heat the butter a little bit to facilitiate the blending of the ingredients. Mix well.

-Store in refrigerator, and use sparingly as a spread.

-Makes 48 servings of 1 tablespoon each.

Substitutions

Instead of olive oil you can use flaxseed oil or another high-omega-3 oil, but if you do, avoid heating it to high heat, such as for stir-frying vegetables. For stir-frying, just use olive oil or coconut oil.

Healthy Tidbit

Toxins such as heavy metals, pesticides, hormones, and antibiotics are stored in the body's fatty tissues. Therefore, it is important to purchase organic sources of foods that are high in fat. This is why only organic butter is allowed on the anti-inflammatory diet. Butter is superior to margarine, because the production of margarine usually involves hydrogenating plant oils to harden them for spreading. The body is physically unable to break down or digest the end results of this process (trans fatty acids).

Poppy Seed Rice

Per Serving: 150.6 Calories ~ 2.1 G Protein ~ 24.3 G Carbohydrate ~ 0.4 G Fiber ~ 4.8 G

Total Fat ~ 0.7 G Saturated Fat ~ 0.0 Mg Cholesterol ~ 0.3 Mg Sodium

This is a fun rice to serve when entertaining. I don't often use basmati rice because the glycemic index is much higher than brown rice, so I save this recipe for special occasions. You can create a very artistic meal using simple ingredients. Avoid this dish if you are diabetic.

Ingredients

- 1 cup basmati rice

- 2 cups filtered water

- 1/2 teaspoon sea salt (optional)

- 2 teaspoons fresh lemon juice

- 6 teaspoons olive oil or olive oil/butter mixture

- 1 teaspoons poppy seeds

- Lemon wedges for garnish

Instructions

*Wash and drain rice. Combine rice, water, sea salt, and lemon juice in a 2- quart saucepan over moderate heat. Bring to a boil.

*In a small skillet, heat the oil over moderate heat; add the poppy seeds, and saute until they become aromatic. Add seeds and oil to the boiling lemon juice, water, and rice; allow the water to fully boil for a few more seconds.

*Reduce the heat to low, cover, and allow the rice to gently simmer without stirring or removing the lid for 15-20 minutes or until the rice is tender, dry, and fluffy. Turn off the heat and set aside for at least 5 minutes before serving.

Serves 6.

Substitutions

You can use brown rice, but it doesn't afford as much color contrast if you are looking for a creative, artistic presentation. It still tastes fabulous, however.

Healthy Tidbit

Poppy seeds are the dried seed of the opium poppy,

Papaver somniferum, an herb native to Greece and the Middle East. Contrary to some myths, the seeds themselves have no narcotic properties. Warming the seeds allows the flavors to come out. Poppy seeds have become popular in many dishes, from rice to salad dressings to sweet muffins. They are about half oil and thus can go rancid rapidly. Once you've opened a sealed container of them, store them in the refrigerator, tightly covered, and use them within a couple of months. To experiment with poppy seeds, try adding % cup to a favorite muffin recipe.

Rosemary Squash

Per Serving: 116.2 Calories ~ 1.4 G Protein ~ 17.8 G Carbohydrate ~ 2.6 G Fiber ~ 5.2 G

Total Fat ~ 0.7 G Saturated Fat ~ 0.0 Mg Cholesterol ~ 116.6 Mg Sodium

Ingredients

- 2-3 small winter squash, such as acorn or spaghetti
- 2 medium sweet potatoes, unpeeled
- 3 tablespoons extra virgin olive oil
- 2 teaspoons rosemary
- 1/2 teaspoon sea salt or to taste
- 1/4 teaspoon pepper or to taste

Instructions

*Cut the squash in half; spoon out the seeds and stringy flesh from the center. Then cut into 3/4-inch chunks, removing the shell.

*Cut the sweet potatoes into 3/4-inch chunks.

Combine sweet potatoes and squash in a large baking pan, drizzle with olive oil, and add seasonings.

*Cover and bake until squash chunks are tender but do not fall apart when you fork them, about 40 minutes. Stir occasionally during the baking process.

Serves 8.

Substitutions

Try many different squash or pumpkin varieties for this dish, and omit the sweet potatoes if you wish.

Healthy Tidbit

In recent years, rosemary has been the subject of research in the arena of cancer prevention,

Alzheimer's prevention and treatment, and heart disease treatment. Studies have shown that rosemary contains more than two dozen antioxidants that may help prevent some of the most serious chronic diseases.

Salad Rolls

Per Serving: 143.8 Calories ~ 11.7 G Protein ~ 11.4 G Carbohydrate ~ 2.2 G Fiber ~ 6.9 G

Total Fat ~ 1.0 G Saturated Fat ~ 0.0 Mg Cholesterol ~ 129.0 Mg Sodium

10 sheets of round rice paper (found in Asian section of the grocery store)

Ingredients

- Small package of rice noodles, cooked and rinsed
- 1 bunch of cilantro, minced or whole, with stems removed
- 1/2 pound of raw firm tofu, cut into long, thin strips
- 2 medium carrots, cut into long, thin strips
- 1/2 cucumber (cut lengthwise), cut into long, thin strips
- Small amount of green leaf lettuce, shredded

Instructions

*Cut cilantro, tofu, carrots, cucumber, and lettuce as directed, and make a pile of each for assembly.

*Cook rice noodles according to package; rinse well with cold water and set aside.

*Fill a large saucepan 1/2 inch to 1 inch deep with filtered water and heat over medium heat. Dip one sheet of rice paper into the water until it softens (about 15-20 seconds). Remove from water, allow excess water to drain off, and transfer to a cutting board.

*One ingredient at a time, arrange a small amount of rice noodles, cilantro, tofu, carrots, cucumbers, and lettuce on the bottom half of the sheet of rice paper. Fold in the sides of the rice paper, and then roll tightly into a large roll and set aside. Repeat with all ten sheets of rice paper.

You will learn how much of each ingredient fits into each roll by experimenting. Cut each roll in half to expose the inside.

Serves 10.

Substitutions

You can make these as simple or complex as you desire. Experiment with different vegetables, or even add leftover fish. Adding fresh mint instead of cilantro also gives a crisp, refreshing taste.

Scrumptious Green Beans

Per Serving: 68.6 Calories ~ 1.5 G Protein ~ 6.5 G Carbohydrate ~ 2.7 G Fiber ~ 4.7 G

Total Fat ~ 0.6 G Saturated Fat ~ 0.0 Mg Cholesterol ~ 393.1 Mg Sodium

Simple green beans never tasted so good. This dish offers a great way to get some green vegetables into your family members' diets.

Ingredients

- 2 tablespoons olive oil
- 1/2 teaspoon black or yellow mustard seeds, available in the bulk herb section of most health-food stores
- 1/2-inch cube of peeled ginger, sliced julienne thin
- 1/4 cup water
- 1 pound green beans, washed and trimmed
- 1/2 teaspoon ground cumin
- 1/4 teaspoon turmeric
- 1 teaspoon sea salt
- 2 tablespoons minced fresh cilantro

- Juice of 1 lemon

Instructions

*Saute mustard seeds and ginger in olive oil over moderate heat until mustard seeds begin to pop.

*Add the beans and stir-fry over medium heat for about 5 minutes. Add the water, cover tightly, and simmer for 5 minutes.

*Remove the lid when most of the water has evaporated.

*Add all remaining ingredients except lemon juice, and continue cooking until the beans are warm but still slightly crispy.

*Add the lemon juice just before serving. Serve warm.

Serves 6.

Simple and Delectable Beets

Per Serving: 26.8 Calories ~ 1.0 G Protein ~ 6.0 G Carbohydrate ~ 1.7 G Fiber ~ 0.1 G

Total Fat ~ 0.0 G Saturated Fat ~ 0.0 Mg Cholesterol ~ 48.0 Mg Sodium

Beets are so sweet that they really need no seasonings. But if you want to experiment with some new flavors, try this recipe.

Ingredients

- 3 beets, peeled and steamed until tender, but still slightly crunchy
- 1 teaspoon lemon juice
- 1 teaspoon honey (optional)
- Sea salt and pepper to taste

Instructions

* Steam beets and set aside to cool slightly.

* Mix lemon juice and honey together over low heat in a 2-quart saucepan until well blended.

* Turn off heat, slice beets, and add them to the pan. *

* Mix gently.

* Add sea salt and pepper to taste, and serve immediately.

* If you are omitting the honey, just slice the cooked beets, sprinkle with lemon juice, sea salt, and pepper, and serve.

Serves 4.

Substitutions

Use a dash of nutmeg or a bit of ginger instead of the honey to add flavor but no sugar.

Breads, Muffins, And Tortillas

Hannah's Rice-Flour Bread

Per Serving: 533.9 Calories ~ 10.2 G Protein ~ 96.7 G Carbohydrate ~ 3.5 G Fiber ~ 12.1 G

Total Fat ~ 6.0 G Saturated Fat ~ 126.1 Mg Cholesterol ~ 740.1 Mg Sodium

Gluten-free bread has never tasted so good. Try this one; you won't be disappointed. This recipe is from Hannah Ashley, a massage therapist practicing in McMinnville, Oregon.

Ingredients

- ½ cup warm water
- 2 teaspoons plus ¼ cup honey
- 4 teaspoons dry yeast granules
- 2 cups rice flour
- 2 cups tapioca flour

- 4 teaspoons xanthan gum, available in health-food stores
- 1¼ teaspoons sea salt
- 1½ cups soy milk
- 4 tablespoons melted organic butter
- 1 teaspoon vinegar
- 3 organic eggs, gently beaten

Instructions

* In a small bowl, mix together water, 2 teaspoons honey, and yeast; set aside for 15 minutes.

* In a large mixing bowl, combine dry ingredients.

* Add wet ingredients to dry ingredients, and stir 20 times.

* Add yeast mixture, and mix all with a mixer/beater. Note: Finished batter looks more like a thick cake batter than bread dough.

* Divide batter into 2 equal amounts. Place in two 8 x 4 x 2½ inch, parchment paper-lined loaf pans. Smooth tops with a wet rubber spatula, and let rise in a warm place for approximately 1 hour.

* Once dough has risen, preheat oven to 350° F. Bake loaves for 20-25 minutes. Serves 6.

Substitutions

You can experiment with different flours for this bread. You can also use any alternative milk in place of the soy milk. coconut oil will easily replace the butter for those who can't tolerate any dairy.

Honey Millet Muffins

Per Serving: 210.1 Calories ~ 5.3 G Protein ~ 35.4 G Carbohydrate ~ 2.7 G Fiber ~ 5.6 G

Total Fat ~ 2.3 G Saturated Fat ~ 26.5 Mg Cholesterol ~ 233.2 Mg Sodium

Ingredients

- 1 organic egg
- 3 tablespoons organic butter, melted
- ½ cup milk substitute (e.g., soy milk) or water
- ½ cup honey
- 2 cups oat flour
- 1 teaspoon baking powder
- ½ teaspoon soda
- ½ teaspoon sea salt
- 1 cup millet, uncooked

- ½ teaspoon guar gum

Instructions

* Preheat oven to 375° F. Mix all wet ingredients together in a large bowl.

* Still mixing, add the dry ingredients slowly. Add millet last, and stir through the mixture.

* Spoon mixture into muffin tin (greased if you are not using paper liners), and bake for 17-20 minutes.

*Makes 12 regular muffins.

Substitutions

This recipe contains enough guar gum to substitute for the gluten in wheat flour, so experiment with substituting different gluten-free flours. oat happens to be my favorite because it tastes similar to whole wheat.

Spelt Tortillas

Per Serving: 140.6 Calories ~ 3.4 G Protein ~ 21.3 G Carbohydrate ~ 3.4 G Fiber ~ 4.2 G

Total Fat ~ 0.5 G Saturated Fat ~ 0.0 Mg Cholesterol ~ 0.1 Mg Sodium

Tortillas can be served with many meals in place of bread or crackers. This wheat-free, corn-free version is fun to make and tastes great.

Ingredients

- 2 cups spelt flour (option: 1 cup white spelt flour, 1 cup whole-grain spelt flour)
- 1 cup warm filtered water (slightly more or less depending on humidity level)
- 2 tablespoons olive oil
- ¼ cup spelt flour (for rolling out the dough)

Instructions

* Add water to spelt flour; knead the dough into a uniform mixture with your hands. Form the mixture into 8 egg-sized balls; set aside for about 20 minutes.

* On a generously floured surface, use a rolling pin to roll out 1 ball into a circle. If the dough sticks to the rolling pin or the surface, add a little more flour. If it falls apart, add a few drops of water.

* Keep rolling the dough until you make a round, very thin tortilla. (As you become more practiced, you will find it easier to make a round shape; it is okay if your tortillas are not perfect the first time around.)

* Heat a skillet over medium-high heat, and add ½ teaspoon olive oil.

Place the tortilla in the skillet, and heat it just enough to lightly brown the bottom (about 60 seconds). When the tortilla is done on one side, it will begin to puff up. Flip the tortilla and heat briefly on the other side until lightly browned (about 60 more seconds).

* Place directly into a napkin and fold the napkin over it to keep it warm. Repeat with each dough ball. Serve immediately.

Makes 8 tortillas

The All-Forgiving Banana Bread

Per Serving: 368.5 Calories ~ 7.0 G Protein ~ 42.3 G Carbohydrate ~ 4.9 G Fiber ~ 20.8 G

Total Fat ~ 6.7 G Saturated Fat ~ 54.5 Mg Cholesterol ~ 232.2 Mg Sodium

Compared to a regular banana bread recipe, it calls for only half the amount of butter/oil because it uses honey instead of sugar. It also contains half the amount of "sugar" of a regular banana bread.

Ingredients

- 1 cup organic butter or vegan margarine (without hydrogenated oils), softened
- 1/8 cup organic coconut oil, warmed to a liquid consistency
- 1 cup honey
- 4 medium ripe bananas, pureed or thoroughly mashed with a fork
- 2 organic eggs
- 1 teaspoon baking soda
- ¼ teaspoon sea salt
- 1 cup chopped walnuts

- 2 cups spelt flour

Instructions

* Preheat oven to 375° F.

* Mix all wet ingredients together. You can use a blender to puree the bananas with the other wet ingredients. Gradually add the dry ingredients to the blender, and mix until smooth.

* Pour into a 9 x 4 x 3-inch greased loaf pan or two small loaf pans. Bake for 15 minutes; reduce oven to 350° F and bake for another 40-45 minutes.

* Makes one 9 x 4-inch loaf (approximately 10 slices).

Substitutions

As always, brown rice syrup is an acceptable substitute for honey. Plus, you can use pretty much any flour, or a combination of flours, and this recipe will turn out

Zucchini Bread

Per Serving: 390.9 Calories ~ 6.7 G Protein ~ 48.3 G Carbohydrate ~ 2.3 G Fiber ~ 20.6 G

Total Fat ~ 15.1 G Saturated Fat ~ 63.5 Mg Cholesterol ~ 272.5 Mg Sodium

Ingredients

- ¾ cup organic coconut oil, warmed to liquid consistency
- 3 organic eggs, beaten

- 2 cups grated zucchini

- 1 cup raw honey

- 1 teaspoon vanilla extract

- 3 cups oat flour

- 1 teaspoon baking soda

- ½ teaspoon sea salt

Instructions

* Preheat oven to 350° F.

* Mix together all wet ingredients, including zucchini. *
Gradually add dry ingredients, mixing thoroughly. Pour
batter into a greased 9 x 4 x 3- inch loaf pan.

* Bake for 1 hour or until a knife inserted in the center
comes out clean. Makes one 9 x 4-inch loaf
(approximately 10 slices).

Substitutions

You can try different combinations of flours with this recipe, but remember, if the flour does not contain gluten, you also need to add a binder. Also experiment with adding seeds, chopped nuts, raisins, etc., for more texture and varied flavor.

Healthy Tidbit

Zucchini are best if you eat them fresh and in season. They are great from mid-summer through late fall. Look for locally grown varieties that are small in size. They can grow quite large, but the larger they get the more their flavor disappears.

When baked into cookies and muffins, zucchini adds moisture and important nutrients.

Breakfasts

Five-Minute Breakfast

PER SERVING: 370.5 CALORIES ~ 11.0 G PROTEIN ~ 40.7 G CARBOHYDRATE ~ 5.2 G FIBER ~ 20.4 G

TOTAL FAT ~ 2.2 G SATURATED FAT ~ 0.0 MG CHOLESTEROL ~ 28.2 MG SODIUM

If you have leftover, cooked brown rice in your refrigerator, this is an easy meal, especially on those mornings when you think there's nothing in your kitchen for breakfast. I always make sure to have nuts, seeds, and raisins on hand for baked goods; therefore I always have the ingredients to make this simple breakfast.

Ingredients

- 1 cup leftover cooked brown rice
- 1 cup sunflower seeds
- 1 teaspoon cinnamon powder
- 1 cup rice milk or other alternative milk
- 1/8 cup raisins

- 1 teaspoon carob powder (optional)

- 1 cup chopped walnuts

- half teaspoon maple syrup (optional)

Instructions

* Combine all ingredients in a saucepan on the stove.

*Add milk to cover the rice for a cereal consistency.

*Warm over moderate heat to desired temperature and serve.

Serves 2.

Substitutions

Any seeds and nuts will do. Experiment with whatever is in your cabinet. pumpkin spice or nutmeg would also be tasty. or add fresh, cut fruit. You can always cook your rice fresh instead of using leftover rice, but the preparation time becomes longer than 5 minutes. Adding coconut milk instead of rice milk is a good way to add more fat to the diet and adds richer flavor.

Healthy Tidbit

Cinnamon-leaf oil can be used for its antiseptic, tonic, and warming properties. It is used to treat nausea and colds, and can be a powerful styptic, which means it can help halt bleeding. Research by Alam Khan and colleagues published in 2003 in the journal Diabetes Care suggests that cinnamon is helpful in regulating and stabilizing blood sugar.

Broccoli and Olive Frittata

PER SERVING: 237.9 CALORIES ~ 15.2 G PROTEIN ~ 14.9 G CARBOHYDRATE ~ 2.3 G FIBER ~ 14.3 G

TOTAL FAT ~ 3.5 G SATURATED FAT ~ 317.3 MG CHOLESTEROL ~ 286.8 MG SODIUM

This is a great-tasting, crustless alternative to quiche.

Ingredients

- 1 medium yellow bell pepper

- 1 medium red bell pepper

- 2 broccoli crowns, cut into bite-size pieces

- 1 cup pitted ripe olives, halved

- 6 organic eggs, softly beaten

- half cup soy milk

- 2 tablespoons chopped fresh sweet basil or

- 1 teaspoon dried basil

- 1 teaspoon dried oregano Sea salt and pepper to taste

- 1 cup cashews, ground fine for garnish

Instructions

* Quarter and seed peppers, then broil them for 5-10 minutes or until lightly charred.

* Place in a closed brown paper bag, and let cool for 5 minutes.

* Peel and thinly slice. (If you don't mind the peel, leave it on and just slice the roasted peppers into thin slices.)

* Reduce oven heat to 400° F.

* Grease a 9-inch round pan. Place broccoli, peppers, and olives in the pan, making sure to arrange them evenly. Beat remaining ingredients together in a small bowl and pour over vegetables.

* Bake for 35-40 minutes or until the center has set. *Broil for the last two minutes to brown the top. Cool, slice into wedges, and serve warm or cold garnished with ground cashews (in place of Parmesan cheese). Serves 4.

Substitutions

You can use this basic recipe for any type of frittata that you desire. Other ingredient ideas include basil, pine nuts, and pesto. You can add spinach to almost any frittata. Be creative.

Granola

PER SERVING: 317.9 CALORIES ~ 7.2 G PROTEIN ~ 24.3 G CARBOHYDRATE ~ 4.7 G FIBER ~ 23.4 G

TOTAL FAT ~ 10.3 G SATURATED FAT ~ 0.0 MG CHOLESTEROL ~ 3.3 MG SODIUM

This simple-to-make version of an old favorite allows you to avoid the additives and hydrogenated oils that are found in most commercially processed granola.

Ingredients

- 6 cups rolled oats
- 1 cup sesame seeds
- 1 cup unsweetened coconut
- half cup honey

- 1 cup chopped almonds

- 1/2 cup organic coconut oil

- 1 cup raw, shelled sunflower seeds

Instructions

* Preheat oven to 325° F.

* Mix dry ingredients together in a large bowl.

* Combine honey and oil in a saucepan and heat to a liquid consistency.

*Pour over dry ingredients.

* Mix well. Flatten into a baking pan.

* Bake for 15-20 minutes. Cool and store in an airtight container. Serve with milk substitute and/or fresh fruit.

Serves 14.

Substitutions

You can prepare this recipe with many different nuts and seeds and even dried fruit if you are not diabetic. For a change I sometimes add V cup of almond butter or tahini. You can also try brown rice syrup instead of honey.

Healthy Tidbit

The botanical name for oats is Avena sativa. One of my favorite medicinal uses for Avena is as an adrenal-supportive herb. It can help increase energy and tonify the adrenals while aiding anxiety or irritability. Because this herb supports the adrenals and energy production, it is an aid in balancing the endocrine system. I also use it for people who have difficulty sleeping related to overactive mind or anxiety. Eating oats has also been known to help decrease cholesterol.

Protein Power Breakfast

PER SERVING: 343.6 CALORIES ~ 10.1 G PROTEIN ~ 30.3 G CARBOHYDRATE ~ 8.8 G FIBER ~ 23.1 G

TOTAL FAT ~ 2.7 G SATURATED FAT ~ 0.0 MG CHOLESTEROL ~ 7.0 MG SODIUM

This quick and easy breakfast is filled with many nutrients, including essential fatty acids and protein.

Ingredients

- 1 tablespoon flaxseeds
- 1 teaspoon honey
- 2 tablespoons sesame seeds
- 1/2 medium banana, sliced
- 2 tablespoons sunflower seeds

Instructions

*Grind all seeds together in your coffee grinder (which by now must be going through an identity crisis).

*Place seeds in a cereal bowl.

* Add honey and a small amount of hot water or hot milk substitute.

*Mix together and top with sliced bananas. Sprinkle a little more honey or maple syrup on top and enjoy.

Serves 1.

Substitutions

According to taste, you can use different combinations of seeds. I also like to add ground coconut. For a cold version of the breakfast, substitute cold milk in place of the hot water.

Quickest Oatmeal You'll Ever Eat

PER SERVING: 297.7 CALORIES ~ 8.2 G PROTEIN ~ 68.4 G CARBOHYDRATE ~ 6.2 G FIBER ~ 4.2 G

TOTAL FAT ~ 0.7 G SATURATED FAT ~ 0.0 MG CHOLESTEROL ~ 196.7 MG SODIUM

This breakfast takes fewer than three minutes to prepare. For an on-the- go version, use a glass bowl with a tightly sealed lid, place all the ingredients in it, and add it to the contents of your briefcase or backpack. If you've used boiling water, when you get to work or school, your cereal will be cool enough to eat.

Ingredients

- 1 cup nut-and-fruit muesli (natural with no additives)
- 1/2-1 cup hot or boiling water
- 1 teaspoon maple syrup (optional; the fruit in the cereal adds

sweetness)

Instructions

78

*Stir all ingredients together in a cereal bowl. Let sit for at least 1 minute before eating.

Serves 1.

Substitutions

Another quick idea for hot cereal is to begin with 1 cup plain oatmeal, add a few frozen berries and a little honey, and pour boiling water over the mix. The water will melt the berries, making the oatmeal ready to eat in about 60 seconds. Adding ground flaxseeds to your oatmeal increases the fiber, protein, and essential fatty acids.

Dr. Fisel's Tofu Scramble

PER SERVING: 140.5 CALORIES ~ 12.1 G PROTEIN ~ 7.0 G CARBOHYDRATE ~ 2.9 G FIBER ~ 8.4 G

TOTAL FAT ~ 1.5 G SATURATED FAT ~ 0.0 MG CHOLESTEROL ~ 277.7 MG SODIUM

I have gained inspiration for many vegetarian dishes from my good friend Matt Fisel, N.D.

Ingredients

- 1 tablespoon olive oil
- 1 onion, chopped
- 1 clove garlic, chopped
- 5 mushrooms, sliced
- 1 cup chopped broccoli
- 1 pound package organic, firm tofu, crumbled
- 2 teaspoons Herbes de Provence
- 1 tablespoon nutritional yeast powder
- 2 teaspoons kelp powder (optional)
- 1 teaspoon cumin powder
- 1 teaspoon cayenne powder (omit if you
- can't tolerate spice)
- 1 tablespoon wheat-free tamari

- Pepper to taste

- Salt to taste

Instructions

* In a large skillet, heat the oil; add the onions, garlic, mushrooms, and broccoli. Saute on medium-high heat until the onions are translucent.

* Add crumbled tofu to pan. Add all of the remaining ingredients and saute until moisture has evaporated and vegetables are tender, about 10 minutes.

Serves 4.

Substitutions

You can use any vegetables for this scramble, even leftover vegetables.

Healthy Tidbit

Tofu, made from soybean curd, is an inexpensive, high-quality source of protein. Soy is a good source of iron, phosphorus, potassium, sodium, and calcium. It also provides B vitamins, choline, and vitamin E

Wheat-Free Pancakes

PER SERVING: 208.1 CALORIES ~ 4.2 G PROTEIN ~ 27.0 G CARBOHYDRATE ~ 2.7 G FIBER ~ 9.4 G

TOTAL FAT ~ 1.0 G SATURATED FAT ~ 0.0 MG CHOLESTEROL ~ 500.95 MG SODIUM

Ingredients

- 1 cup walnuts, ground in food processor to a fine powder
- ½ cup spelt flour
- ½ cup rice flour
- 1 teaspoon cream of tartar
- 1 teaspoon baking soda
- 1/2 teaspoon sea salt
- 1 cup water
- 1 tablespoon olive oil

Instructions

* Optional—sprinkle fresh berries, chopped apple, or chopped nuts into batter.

* Combine ground walnuts, flours, salt, cream of tartar, baking soda, and salt in a medium-sized mixing bowl, blending well.

* Whisk 1 cup of water into dry ingredients, then gradually add the rest of the water to reach desired consistency. Add more water if the bat-ter is still too thick.

* Stir in any optional ingredients until just combined.

Brush or spray a large skillet or griddle with small amount of oil. Heat skillet or griddle over medium heat.

* Drop batter onto hot cooking surface using a large spoon. Cook the pancake until bubbles form on top; flip. Cook on the second side until lightly browned.

Serves 6.

Substitutions

You can try other nuts (e.g., pecans) and other types of flour. If you replace the spelt flour with a nongluten flour, you may need to add V-V teaspoon guar gum or a blended banana.

Easy Pancakes

PER SERVING: 322.7 CALORIES ~ 18.4 G PROTEIN ~ 15.9 G CARBOHYDRATE ~ 2.7 G FIBER ~ 21.6 G

TOTAL FAT ~ 4.4 G SATURATED FAT ~ 317.3 MG CHOLESTEROL ~ 120.7 MG SODIUM

These pancakes, which have a delicious nutty flavor, offer a high amount of fiber and can be made with virtually no flour.

Ingredients

- 3 tablespoons raw sunflower seeds, ground fine
- 3 tablespoons raw pumpkin seeds, ground fine 3 organic eggs
- 1 cup nongluten oat flour (any nonwheat or nongluten flour will do)
- 1 cup rice milk
- 1/2 cup blueberries (optional)

Imstruction

*Combine all ingredients in a medium-sized bowl and mix well until clumps have dissolved.

*Heat a lightly oiled skillet or griddle pan over medium heat.

* Pour batter into 3-inch diameter circles in the pan.

*When pancakes begin to bubble, flip and cook on the other side for a short amount of time until lightly browned on both sides.

Serves 2.

Breakfast Eggnog

PER SERVING: 303.3 CALORIES ~ 19.6 G PROTEIN ~ 20.4 G CARBOHYDRATE ~ 0.0 G FIBER ~ 12.9 G

TOTAL FAT ~ 3.6 G SATURATED FAT ~ 423.0 MG CHOLESTEROL ~ 226.1 MG SODIUM

This is a very easy breakfast to whip together for yourself or your children and offers a good source of complete protein in the morning.

- *2 organic eggs*
- *1 cup rice milk, chilled*
- *1 tablespoon vanilla extract Dash cinnamon Dash nutmeg*

Combine all ingredients in a large cup or bowl, and mix well until mixture looks uniform.

Strain mixture through small strainer into a serving glass and serve. Serves 1.

Substitutions

Soy milk or another alternate milk can be used in place of rice milk.

Vegemite on Toast

Ingredients

- 2 slices bread, preferable white

- 1/8 teaspoon vegemite, more if you are game

- 1/2 teaspoon butter or 1/2 teaspoon margarine

Directions

First of all, toast a bread and butter it.

Then after this, spread a fine layer of vegemite over it.

Banana Nut Bread

Ingredients

- 3 cups flour 3/4 teaspoon salt
- 1 teaspoon baking soda 2 cups sugar 1 teaspoon cinnamon 3 eggs
- 1 cup oil
- 2 cups mashed bananas (ripe) 1 (8 ounce) cans crushed pineapple with juice 1 teaspoon vanilla
- 1/2-1 cup chopped walnuts

Directions

First of all, blend the eggs, oil and sugar in a bowl.

Then add the remaining items besides nuts and blend well.

Then blend in nuts.

Bake for approximately 1 hour at THREE HUNDRED FIFTY (35^0) degrees Fahrenheit or till ready and done.

Breakfast on an English Muffin

Ingredients

- 4 English muffins or 8 crumpets, cut in half 1/3 cup peanut butter

- 1/3 cup honey 2 bananas, thinly sliced 1/8 teaspoon cinnamon

Directions

First of all, slightly toast the muffins.

Take peanut butter and spread this over the muffins.

Then spread honey over the muffins.

Use the bananas for topping.

Then grill till honey sizzles.

Use cinnamon as sprinkle.

Cinnamon and Raisin Oats

Ingredients

- 250 ml skim milk (1 cup)

- 1 tablespoon sugar

- 45 g instant oats (1/2 cup)

- 1 1/2 tablespoons raisins 1/2 teaspoon cinnamon

  ground cinnamon, extra to serve (optional)

Directions

- Take the milk and mix it with sugar in saucepan

  and heat to boiling over moderate temperature.

- Blend in oats. Blend in raisins. Blend in cinnamon.

- Cook, mixing from time to time, for THREE min or

  till become thick.

- Then distribute into bowls and use additional cinnamon as sprinkle.

Cheese & Bacon Breakfast Muffins

Ingredients

- 3 slices bacon (rind removed and chopped)

- 1 tablespoon olive oil 400 g button mushrooms (finely chopped)

- 1 1/2 cups plain flour

- 3 teaspoons baking powder

- 1/4 teaspoon salt (freshly ground)

- 1/4 teaspoon black pepper (freshly ground)

- 1 cup cheese (grated)

- 2 tablespoons chives (finely chopped) 80 g butter (melted)

- 2 eggs (lightly whisked)

- 2/3 cup milk

Directions

- First of all, saute the bacon over moderately high temperature setting in saute pan till golden in color, mixing from time to time.
- Then shift to paper towel.
- Add the oil and mushrooms to saute pan and cook for FIVE min over high temperature setting till soft.
- Then put aside.
- Grease a TWELVE holes muffin tin.
- Take the flour, baking powder and sift these items with salt and pepper in a bowl and then add in cheese.
- Then add in chives and blend them well.

Take the butter and whisk with egg and milk in jug and pour this over dry items, mixing till mixed.

Then right after this, fold through bacon and mushrooms.

Take mixture and spoon this into pan.

Bake for approximately 1/3 hour at TWO HUNDRED degrees Celsius.

Pacific Style Omelet

Ingredients

- 6 large eggs

- 1 medium potato, grated

- 1 tablespoon parsley, diced 100 g ham, Virginian sliced and diced

- 1/4 teaspoon ground black pepper

- 1/4 teaspoon sage

- 1 medium onion, finely diced

- 1 tablespoon butter

- 2 button mushrooms, sliced

- 2 cherry tomatoes, sliced

- 1/4 green capsicum, diced (green pepper)

- 1/4 red capsicum, diced (red pepper)

- 2 teaspoons parmesan cheese 100 g cream cheese, finely diced

Directions

- Take the eggs and whisk them in bowl.

- Take the grated potato, onion, sage, parsley, ham, pepper and add them to bowl and blend them.

- Add the mixture to melted butter in pan over moderate temperature so it begin bubbling.

- Take the mushrooms, tomato, cheese, capsicum and spread them over.

- Cook for approximately 1/2 hour or till top begins to get firm.

- Chop in half, don't fold.

Lemonade Scones

Ingredients

- 1 cup heavy cream

- 1 cup lemonade

- 3 cups self-rising flour

- 1 pinch salt jam, to serve cream, to serve

Directions

- Blend everything together in a bowl.

- Then knead and shape the dough out to approximately ONE inch thick.

- After this, chop out scones by using round shape cutter.

- Then put them on cookie sheet that has been greased.

- Use milk for brushing the tops.

- Then bake for approximately ^ hour at FOUR HUNDRED FIFTY degrees Fahrenheit or till top become brown in color.
- You can serve this delicious recipe with cream and jam.

Asparagus Omelette Wraps

Ingredients

- 8 eggs
- 1/2 cup milk
- 1 tablespoon fresh sage, roughly chopped
- 1 teaspoon fresh thyme, chopped
- 2 garlic cloves, chopped
- 1/4 cup pecorino cheese, grated
- 24 stalks asparagus
- 2 tablespoons extra virgin olive oil

Directions

- Take eggs and beat them in bowl.

- Take milk, sage and add them to bowl along with pecorino, garlic and thyme. Then use the cracked black pepper for seasoning.

- After this, layer the asparagus in pan with enough salted and boiling water in order to cover spears.

- Cook for 120 seconds till soft however yet crunchy.

- After this, pour a ladle of egg mixture in little bit heated olive oil in heated saute pan and roll the pan around till egg is finely layered over base and cooked on one side.

Crumpets With Cheese & Bacon

Ingredients

- 4 crumpets

- 1/4 cup cheddar cheese, grated

- 50 g bacon (one large slice or rasher)

- 1/4 teaspoon ground pepper (optional)

- 1/4 teaspoon ground paprika (optional)

Directions

- First of all, cook the bacon in skillet and put aside.

- Use the cheese as sprinkle all over every crumpet and then sprinkle the pepper and paprika.

- Then after this, tear up the bacon and put over top and remove the fat and rind. Then grill for approximately TEN min or till cheese melts into crumpet.

Chicken Stew

Ingredients

- 1/4 cup oil

- 1 cup chopped onion

- 1 (14 ounce) cans diced tomatoes

- 2 cups chicken broth

- 1 teaspoon minced garlic

- 1 teaspoon thyme

- 1 bay leaf

- 1 teaspoon salt

- 1/2 teaspoon pepper

- 4 cups diced potatoes

- 1 1/2 cups sliced carrots

- 2 cups chopped chicken breasts

Directions

- Fry the onion in oil in pot for 120 seconds.

- Add the following SEVEN items.

- Heat to boiling.

- Take potatoes, chicken, carrots and add them.

- Allow to simmer till veggies are ready and done, approximately V hour. Use the cornstarch for thickening the stew.

Parmesan Crusted Broiled Scallops

Ingredients

- 1/3 cup finely crushed onion flavored melba toast, about 9

- 1 tablespoon grated parmesan cheese

- 1 tablespoon minced fresh parsley

- 1/4 teaspoon paprika

- 1 1/2 lbs sea scallops

- 1 tablespoon butter, melted lemon wedge

Directions

- Mix the 1st FOUR items and ONE FOURTH tsp of black pepper in Ziploc plastic bag.

- Use the butter for brushing the scallops.

- Then add them to bag and seal the bag and shake well.

- Put the scallops on broiler pan sprayed with cooking oil.

- Then broil for TEN min or till ready and done.

- You can serve this delicious recipe with lemon wedges.

Easy Pork Chops

Ingredients

- 1/2 teaspoon salt

- 1/4 teaspoon pepper

- 1/4 teaspoon paprika

- 1/4 teaspoon sage

- 1/4 teaspoon thyme

- 4 boneless pork loin chops

- 1 tablespoon oil 1 onion, sliced

Directions

- Blend dry items and sprinkle on each of the side of pork chops. After this, cook the chops in oil.

- Then put every chop on heavy foil piece.

- After this, layer each one with onions.

- After this, seal the pouches.

- Then put on baking sheet.

Entrees

Amaranth

Per Serving: 182.3 Calories ~ 7.0 G Protein ~ 32.3 G Carbohydrate ~ 4.5 G Fiber

~ 3.2 G

Total Fat ~ 0.8 G Saturated Fat ~ 0.0 Mg Cholesterol ~ 10.2 Mg Sodium

Amaranth does not contain any gluten and thus is recommended for people who can't tolerate that protein. It is rich in lysine, an essential amino acid that many grains lack.

Ingredients

- 1 cup amaranth cups filtered water

Instructions

- place water and amaranth in a 2-quart saucepan.
- Bring to boil, reduce heat to low, cover, and simmer for 20-25 minutes. Yields 2 cups. Serves 4.

Barley

PER SERVING: 93.1 CALORIES ~ 3.3 G PROTEIN ~ 19.3 G CARBOHYDRATE ~ 4.5 G FIBER ~ 0.6 G

TOTAL FAT ~ 0.1 G SATURATED FAT ~ 0.0 MG CHOLESTEROL ~ 3.2 MG SODIUM

Barley has a really good texture for soups and cereal. Buy nonpearled (unhulled) barley because pearling removes more than 30 percent of the grain's nutrition.

Ingredients

- 1 cup barley
- 3 cups filtered water

Place water and barley in a 2-quart saucepan. Bring to boil, reduce heat to low, cover, and simmer for 1 hour and 15 minutes. Alternatively, place all ingredients in a crockpot and simmer on high for about 3 hours.

Serves 7.

You can grind your own flour from barley, which can be used to make gravies or can be added to other flours to make baked goods and breads.

Brown Rice

PER SERVING: 114.1 CALORIES ~ 2.4 G PROTEIN ~ 23.8 G CARBOHYDRATE ~ 1.1 G FIBER ~ 0.9 G

TOTAL FAT ~ 0.2 G SATURATED FAT ~ 0.0 MG CHOLESTEROL ~ 2.2 MG SODIUM

- 1 cup brown rice, short or long grain
- 2 cups filtered water

Place water and rice in a 2- quart saucepan. Bring to boil; immediately reduce heat to low. Simmer, covered, for 30-40 minutes or until all water has been absorbed. Yields 3 cups. Serves 6.

Millet

PER SERVING: 108.0 CALORIES ~ 3.1 G PROTEIN ~ 20.8 G CARBOHYDRATE ~ 2.4 G FIBER ~ 1.2 G

TOTAL FAT ~ 0.2 G SATURATED FAT ~ 0.0 MG CHOLESTEROL ~ 1.4 MG SODIUM

Millet can be used in place of rice or quinoa. It adds a crunchy texture to salads and vegetable dishes.

- 1 cup millet
- 3 cups filtered water

Place water and millet in a 2-quart saucepan. Bring to boil, reduce heat to low, cover, and simmer for 35-40 minutes. Yields 3 cups

Oats

PER SERVING: 202.3 CALORIES ~ 8.8 G PROTEIN ~ 34.5 G CARBOHYDRATE ~ 5.5 G FIBER ~ 3.6 G

TOTAL FAT ~ 0.6 G SATURATED FAT ~ 0.0 MG CHOLESTEROL ~ 1.0 MG SODIUM

Oats are sadly underused. Don't just think of them as oatmeal. You can add them to soups and casseroles for a little extra body, or to cookies or other baked goods.

- 1 cup oats
- 2 cups filtered water

Place water and oats in a 2- quart saucepan. cook over low heat for 20-25 minutes. Yields 2 cups.

Serves 3.

Quinoa

PER SERVING: 127.2 CALORIES ~ 4.5 G PROTEIN ~ 23.4 G CARBOHYDRATE ~ 2.0 G FIBER ~ 2.0 G

TOTAL FAT ~ 0.2 G SATURATED FAT ~ 0.0 MG CHOLESTEROL ~ 7.1 MG SODIUM

One of my favorite grains, quinoa is very low in gluten. It complements many salads, stir-fries, burgers, egg dishes, meat dishes—just about anything. it is higher in protein than any other grain, and its protein is a complete protein, meaning it contains all of the essential amino acids, a quality shared by very few plant-based foods.

- 1 cup quinoa
- 2 cups filtered water

place water and quinoa in a 2-quart saucepan. Bring to boil and then immediately reduce heat to low.

Simmer, covered, for 10-15 minutes or until all water has been absorbed.

Yields 3 cups. Serves 5.

Salads

Basil & Tomato Salad

Ingredients

- 4 Tomatoes
- 1/4 cup basil leaves, torn
- 1 -2 tablespoon olive oil
- fresh ground black pepper
- sea salt

Directions

First of all, horizontally chop the tomatoes into slices.

Then organize on a dish.

Use the oil to drizzle and after this, scatter the basil leaves all over.

Add the salt and pepper as seasonings.

Pea Salad

Ingredients

- 1 (500 g) packets frozen baby peas, thawed, drained 1/2 cup finely chopped red onion

- 1/2 cup diced cooked bacon

- 1/2 cup corn kernel

- 1 cup grated tasty cheddar cheese

- 1/2 cup diced red capsicum (bell pepper)

- 1/4 cup sour cream

- 1/4 cup mayonnaise

- salt & freshly ground black pepper

Directions

Blend all of the above items in a bowl.

Keep in refrigerator for chilling for a few hrs.

Creamy Feta Salad Dressing and Dip

Ingredients

- 5 ounces feta cheese

- 1/4 cup buttermilk or 1/4 cup milk

- 1/2 cup sour cream

- 1/2 cup mayonnaise

- 2 tablespoons white wine vinegar

- 2 cloves garlic, finely minced

- 1 green onion, finely chopped

- 1 teaspoon chopped fresh dill

- 1 teaspoon dried oregano salt and pepper

Directions

First of all, mash buttermilk and cheese together till look

like the cottage cheese consistency.

Then blend in the rest of items.

After this, add the salt and pepper according to your own choice.

Allow to rest in refrigerator, covered, for a minimum of a couple of hrs

Coleslaw

Ingredients

- 1/2 cabbage, shredded

- 1 onion, finely sliced

- 1 carrot, shredded

- 1/3 cup milk

- 1/2 cup mayonnaise

- 1/4 cup sugar

- 2 tablespoons vinegar

- 2 tablespoons lemon juice salt,

- pepper

Directions

Take the 1st THREE items and add them to a bowl.

Blend the rest of items in s sauce.

Then pour over the vegetables.

Blend completely and keep in refrigerator for a minimum of THREE hrs

Home-Grown Alfalfa Sprouts

PER SERVING: 9.6 CALORIES ~ 1.3 G PROTEIN ~ 1.2 G CARBOHYDRATE ~ 0.9 G FIBER ~ 0.2 G TOTAL

FAT ~ 0.0 G SATURATED FAT ~ 0.0 MG CHOLESTEROL ~ 2.0 MG SODIUM

Sprouts are so easy to grow, taste delicious, and offer a large amount of the enzymes needed to aid in digestion. You can add them to salads, stir- fries, and many other meals.

121

Ingredients

- 1/3 cup alfalfa seeds
- Filtered water

Special equipment:

- Large Mason jar
- Cheesecloth

Instructions

Place the seeds in the jar. Add enough filtered water to cover the seeds. Cover the top with 2-3 thicknesses of cheesecloth, and secure with a strong rubber band or with the metal rim that fits the jar.

Place the jar in a warm place away from direct sunlight. Let the seeds soak for 6-8 hours.

After this initial soaking, rinse the seeds through the cheesecloth. Drain out excess water. Then turn the jar upside down and place it on a plate; this allows the water to drain. Rinse 3-4 times per day. Sprouts should be ready to eat in about 4 days.

Serves 1.

Avocado Tuna Salad

PER SERVING: 222.7 CALORIES ~ 30.1 G PROTEIN ~ 4.9 G CARBOHYDRATE ~ 3.8 G FIBER ~ 9.2 G

TOTAL FAT ~ 1.5 G SATURATED FAT ~ 34.0 MG CHOLESTEROL ~ 387.3 MG SODIUM

Try this salad when you want a nutritious, tasty lunch and don't have much time for preparation.

Ingredients

- 1 ripe medium avocado

- 2 6-ounce cans of light tuna, in water

- 1 teaspoon sea salt (optional)

- 1 teaspoon pepper Mash avocado.

Instruction

Add tuna and pepper.

Mix together, and serve on rice crackers, salad greens, or nonwheat bread. My favorite is to serve it over lettuce leaves.

Serves 3.

Substitutions

Canned salmon can be used in place of canned tuna. You can add a little cumin, thyme, or dried basil.

Beet and Bean Salad

PER SERVING: 215.5 CALORIES ~ 5.4 G PROTEIN ~ 21.4 G CARBOHYDRATE ~ 5.3 G FIBER ~ 13.2 G

TOTAL FAT ~ 1.6 G SATURATED FAT ~ 0.0 MG CHOLESTEROL ~ 58.0 MG SODIUM

This delicious, nutritious salad offers a nice change of pace. When I made it for a holiday dinner it was quickly gobbled down.

For the salad:

- 1 cup hazelnuts
- 3-4 large beets, steamed until tender and peeled

- 2 cups green beans, cut into bite size pieces and steamed until tender

- 1 cup cooked white beans

- 1 pear, cut into thin slices

- 1 leek, sliced (mostly the white part)

For the dressing:

- 2 tablespoons fresh dill or 1 teaspoon dry dill

- 2 cloves garlic, minced

- 2 teaspoons mustard, no additives or sugar

- 2 teaspoons balsamic vinegar

- 1 cup extra-virgin olive oil

Instructions

Cut cooked beets into bite-size pieces and combine in a large bowl with green beans, white beans, pear slices, and leek slices.

Prepare dressing by whisking all ingredients together in a small bowl. Pour over salad, mix well, and store in refrigerator for at least 1 hour before serving.

Roast hazelnuts on a cake pan in the oven until golden, about 6-8 minutes. Remove from oven, allow to cool slightly, chop, and set aside until salad is finished marinating. Sprinkle hazelnuts over salad before serving.

Serves 6.

Garlic Bean Salad

PER SERVING: 101.1 CALORIES ~ 2.2 G PROTEIN ~ 8.8 G CARBOHYDRATE ~ 3.9 G FIBER ~ 7.2 G

TOTAL FAT ~ 1.0 G SATURATED FAT ~ 0.0 MG CHOLESTEROL ~ 7.3 MG SODIUM

Here is another great recipe from acupuncturist Dawn Berry, L.Ac.

- 1 pound green beans, blanched and cooled
- 2 tablespoons olive oil
- 2 teaspoons apple cider vinegar
- 1 teaspoon thyme
- 1 garlic clove, minced
- 1 small shallot, minced
- Sea salt and pepper to taste

Prepare the beans by blanching in steam for 2-3 minutes until they are bright green. Set aside to cool.

Whisk together remaining ingredients, and toss with cooled green beans. Place in refrigerator to marinate for 1 hour before serving.

Serves 4.

Carrot Beet Salad

PER SERVING: 156.1 CALORIES ~ 2.1 G PROTEIN ~ 13.0 G CARBOHYDRATE ~ 2.7 G FIBER ~ 11.4 G

TOTAL FAT ~ 1.6 G SATURATED FAT ~ 0.0 MG CHOLESTEROL ~ 329.8 MG SODIUM

For the dressing:

- 4 tablespoons apple cider vinegar

- 3 tablespoons olive oil

- 2 tablespoons mustard (select one containing no additives or sugar)

- 1½ teaspoon sea salt or to taste

- 1½ teaspoon pepper or to taste

- For the salad:

- ½ pound carrots, grated

- 3 raw beets, peeled and grated

Mix dressing ingredients together; taste, and adjust seasonings as you desire. Add grated beets and grated carrots; toss to coat with dressing. Serve chilled.

Serves 4.

Substitutions

You could try different salad dressings. You could also add a few grated radishes for a hint of spice.

Soups

Clean-Out-the-Refrigerator Soup

PER SERVING: 341.7 CALORIES ~ 26.6 G PROTEIN ~ 46.5 G CARBOHYDRATE ~ 10.2 G FIBER ~ 5.7 G

TOTAL FAT ~ 1.3 G SATURATED FAT ~ 36.3 MG CHOLESTEROL ~ 742.0 MG SODIUM

All of the ingredients listed below are optional; they are merely suggestions to get you started.

For the broth:

- 6 cups organic chicken stock
- 1 onion, minced
- 3 garlic cloves, minced or pressed
- 2 tablespoons garlic bean sauce (from Asian section of supermarket)
- 2 tablespoons miso soup paste
- Herbs, spices, and sea salt to taste

Additional ingredients:

- 1 cup oats, ground in a coffee grinder or blender (for a thickener)
- 1 cup lentils, soaked overnight and water discarded
- 3 large carrots, sliced
- 3 celery stalks, sliced
- 1 large zucchini, sliced
- 10 shiitake mushrooms, sliced
- 1 medium sweet potato, cubed
- 2 cups leftover boneless, skinless chicken

The key to a good-tasting soup is to get the broth right before adding vegetables and/or meat. Before turning on the stove, taste the broth cold and adjust the seasonings.

Start by combining chicken stock with onions and garlic in a soup pot.

Add herbs, spices, garlic bean sauce, miso, or anything else you desire.

When the taste meets your satisfaction, turn the burner to medium high, bring the broth to a boil, then immediately reduce heat and simmer for 15 minutes, covered. Keep tasting and adding seasonings as desired.

For a thicker broth, you can add ground oats at this time. Also add legumes. Don't use too many of these ingredients, because they are dense. Simmer, covered, for another 15 minutes.

Add vegetables, and simmer, covered, for another 15 minutes. Add leftover meat and simmer, covered, for another 15-30 minutes.

After the vegetables have cooked to your satisfaction, turn off the heat and allow the soup to sit covered for at least 15 minutes before serving; this step allows the flavors to mingle. Serve plain or with rice crackers.

Serves 6.

Cream of Carrot and Ginger Soup

PER SERVING: 289.9 CALORIES ~ 4.8 G PROTEIN ~ 25.0 G CARBOHYDRATE ~ 5.2 G FIBER ~ 19.8 G

TOTAL FAT ~ 11.3 G SATURATED FAT ~ 0.0 MG CHOLESTEROL ~ 418.1 MG SODIUM

- 2 pounds organic carrots

- 6 garlic cloves

- 2 medium yellow onions

- 2 tablespoons olive oil

- 2 cups organic chicken broth

- 1 cups coconut milk

- 1/3 cup soy milk

- 2 teaspoons grated fresh ginger

- 1 teaspoon sea salt

- 1 teaspoon pepper

- 2 tablespoons dried parsley (as garnish)

- Steam the carrots until soft.

While the carrots are steaming, saute the garlic and onions in the olive oil until they are softened and slightly brown in color.

Combine steamed carrots, cooked garlic and onions, and all remaining ingredients in a blender. Blend on the puree setting. (Caution: Don't heat the liquid ingredients before blending. Using a blender to mix large quantities of hot liquids can cause a rapid expansion in the liquids, which can create a small explosion! If you have to blend hot liquids in a blender, do so in several small batches.)

Heat the blended soup in a large saucepan, and serve garnished with dried parsley. Serves 6.

Dr. Fisel's Squash Soup

PER SERVING: 172.1 CALORIES ~ 2.8 G PROTEIN ~ 32.7 G CARBOHYDRATE ~ 5.2 G FIBER ~ 4.1 G

TOTAL FAT ~ 0.6 G SATURATED FAT ~ 0.0 MG CHOLESTEROL ~ 562.5 MG SODIUM

- 1 medium onion, chopped
- 1 tablespoon olive oil
- 2 cups vegetable stock
- 2 cups butternut squash (seeds removed), peeled and diced
- 2 cups sweet potatoes or yams, peeled and diced
- 1 apple, cored and diced
- 1 teaspoon freshly grated ginger
- 1 teaspoon nutmeg
- 1 teaspoon salt
- 1/2 teaspoon pepper
- 1 teaspoon cayenne pepper

139

In a large soup pot, saute the onions in oil on medium-high heat until translucent.

Add all other ingredients and bring to a boil.

Turn down heat and simmer for 30 minutes.

Remove 2 ladles of vegetables and 1 ladle of stock; puree them together in a blender or food processor until smooth. Return to soup pot; stir soup before serving.

Serves 4.

Nutty Onion Soup

PER SERVING: 543.1 CALORIES ~ 12.5 G PROTEIN ~ 33.9 G CARBOHYDRATE ~ 4.4 G FIBER ~ 43.1 G

TOTAL FAT ~ 7.7 G SATURATED FAT ~ 0.0 MG CHOLESTEROL ~ 475.1 MG SODIUM

- 1 quart of organic chicken broth

- 1 cups filtered water

- 2 cups cashews

- 2 small onions, chopped

- 3 tablespoons cold-pressed, extra-virgin olive oil

- 2 teaspoons marjoram

- 2 teaspoons thyme

- 1 tablespoon chives, minced (for garnish)

Grind the nuts in a coffee grinder until very fine.

In a large skillet, saute the onions in oil on medium-high heat until translucent. Remove from heat and allow to cool slightly.

Transfer the nuts and onions to a blender with remaining ingredients and blend until smooth.

Transfer to a soup pot and simmer on medium heat for 20-30 minutes. Serve warm, garnished with minced chives.

Serves 4.

Raw Beet Soup

PER SERVING: 237.8 CALORIES ~ 4.5 G PROTEIN ~ 30.7 G CARBOHYDRATE ~ 8.4 G FIBER ~ 12.6 G

TOTAL FAT ~ 1.8 G SATURATED FAT ~ 0.0 MG CHOLESTEROL ~ 168.0 MG SODIUM

- 3 medium organic beets (enough to obtain 1 cup juice)
- 1 pound organic carrots (enough to obtain 1 cup juice)
- 1 cup chopped green onion
- 1 cup shredded green cabbage
- 1 teaspoon chopped dill
- 1/2 cup finely grated beets
- 1 large avocado, spooned into chunks
- 1/2 apple, thinly sliced

Put beets and carrots through juicer to yield one cup of each. (You can buy fresh juice at a health-food store or juice bar if you do not have a juicer.)

Place all ingredients except avocado, grated beets, and apple into the blender, and blend until smooth.

Chill until ready to serve. Serve cold garnished with avocados, beets, and apple.

10-Minute Avocado Soup

PER SERVING: 797.5 CALORIES ~ 26.7 G PROTEIN ~ 30.2 G CARBOHYDRATE ~ 17.6 G FIBER ~ 69.9

G TOTAL FAT ~ 6.2 G SATURATED FAT ~ 0.0 MG CHOLESTEROL ~ 329.1 MG SODIUM

This soup is easy to make, tastes great, and fills the stomach on a cool night.

- 2 medium ripe avocados
- 2 cups almond milk

- 1 teaspoon cumin

- 1 teaspoon ground ginger

- 1 teaspoon salt

- 1 clove garlic, minced

- Mash avocados in a pan.

Add all remaining ingredients. Stir well until mixed fully.

You may use an electric beater or blender for this step.

When the soup is well mixed, heat just enough to serve.

Serves 4.

Smoothies

Banana

Blend 2 bananas, 1/2 cup each vanilla yogurt and milk, 2 teaspoons honey, a pinch of cinnamon and 1 cup ice.

Strawberry-Banana

Blend 1 banana, 1 cup strawberries, 1/2 cup each vanilla yogurt and milk, 2 teaspoons honey, a pinch of cinnamon and 1 cup ice.

Strawberry Shortcake

Blend 2 cups strawberries, 1 cup crumbled pound cake, 1 1/2 cups each milk and ice, and sugar to taste. Top with whipped cream and more strawberries.

Triple-Berry

Blend 1 1/2 cups mixed blackberries, strawberries and raspberries with 1 cup each milk and ice, and sugar to taste.

Raspberry-Orange

Blend 1 cup each orange juice and raspberries, 1/2 cup plain yogurt, 1 cup ice, and sugar to taste.

Peach-Mango-Banana

Blend 1 cup each chopped fresh or frozen peaches and mango, 1 cup each plain yogurt and ice, 1/2 banana, and sugar to taste.

Honeydew-Almond

Blend 2 cups chopped honeydew melon, 1 cup each almond milk and ice, and honey to taste.

Cantaloupe

Blend 2 cups chopped cantaloupe, the juice of 1/2 lime, 3 tablespoons sugar, 1/2 cup water and 1 cup ice.

Carrot-Apple

Blend 1 cup each carrot juice and apple juice with 1 1/2 cups ice.

Spa Cucumber

Peel, seed and chop 2 medium cucumbers. Blend with the juice of 1 lime, 1/2 cup water, 1 cup ice and 3 to 4 tablespoons sugar or honey.

Kiwi-Strawberry

Blend 1 cup strawberries, 2 peeled kiwis, 2 tablespoons sugar and 2 cups ice.

Cherry-Vanilla

Blend 1 1/2 cups frozen pitted cherries, 1 1/4 cups milk, 3 tablespoons sugar, 1/2 teaspoon vanilla extract, 1/4 teaspoon almond extract, a pinch of salt and 1 cup ice.

Tangerine-Honey

Peel and seed 4 tangerines, then blend with the juice of 2 limes, 1/4 cup honey and 1 cup ice.

Apricot-Almond

Blend 1 1/2 cups apricot nectar, 1/2 cup vanilla yogurt, 2 tablespoons almond butter and 1 cup ice.

Grape

Blend 2 cups seedless red grapes with 1 cup concord grape juice and 1 1/2 cups ice.

Blueberry-Pear

Blend 1 1/2 cups frozen blueberries, 1 chopped pear, 1 1/2 cups each maple or plain yogurt and ice, and sugar to taste.

Banana-Date-Lime

Blend 2 bananas, 3/4 cup chopped pitted dates, the juice of 1 lime and 1 1/2 cups each soy milk and ice.

Peach-Ginger

Blend 2 cups frozen sliced peaches, 1 1/2 cups buttermilk, 3 tablespoons brown sugar and 1 tablespoon grated fresh ginger.

Grapefruit

Peel and seed 2 grapefruits, then blend with 3 to 4 tablespoons sugar and 1 cup ice. Sprinkle with cinnamon.

Pomegranate-Cherry

Blend 1 cup frozen pitted cherries, 3/4 cup pomegranate juice, 1/2 cup plain yogurt, 1 tablespoon honey, 1 teaspoon lemon juice, a pinch each of cinnamon and salt, and 2 cups ice.

Made in the USA
Monee, IL
26 March 2021